Introducing Patchwork

Introducing Patchwork

Alice Timmins

B. T. Batsford Limited London
Watson-Guptill Publications New York

First published 1968
Library of Congress Catalog Card Number 68-18705
(U.K.) ISBN 0-7134-2656 x
(U.S.) ISBN 0-8230-6270 8

Printed and bound in Denmark by
F. E. Bording Limited, Copenhagen and London
for the Publishers
B. T. Batsford Limited
4 Fitzhardinge Street London W. 1 and
Watson-Guptill Publications
165 West 46th Street, New York NY10036

First Printing, 1968
Second Printing, 1972

Contents

Acknowledgment

I acknowledge with gratitude the help of Harry Timmins, who took all the photographs except those on pages 75, 76 and 95; Annie Barnes, Jessie Doodson, Joan M.F. Louden, Eirian Short, Marjorie Timmins, and students at the Training Centre, Kirkham, who allowed me to use illustrations of their work; Ita Caunce and Pauline Green, who experimented with patchwork so enthusiastically and whose first efforts are shown; Frederick Hankes, FALPA, FRVA, who drew the diagrams for templates; Catherine Timmins who typed the manuscript.

Chorley, Lancashire 1968   A.T.

Introduction

Patchwork is one of the most inexpensive of all crafts; the tools needed are few and the fabrics cost little or nothing.

It can be of great value in education. It is creative and can teach a great deal about colour and design in an interesting and practical way. Children can be brought to appreciate the necessity for accuracy and firm construction, and they will more willingly acquire the techniques of tacking (basting), seaming and sewing by machine when they realise that these are necessary steps to a desirable end. The possibilities for co-operative work are many.

Patchwork is not an isolated needlecraft activity in school; the fitting together of shapes and the construction of templates are mathematical problems to be solved, the washing and dyeing of fabric is part of the domestic science course, while the knowledge of colour and design to be gained is a contribution to education in art. It has a therapeutic value too, as the rhythmic action of seaming can be very soothing.

Much traditional patchwork has qualities of vitality, spontaneity and unselfconscious charm. This is partly due to the fact that every available scrap of fabric had to be used to make articles of everyday use which were urgently needed.

Today, when fabrics are plentiful, there is a danger that these qualities may be lost. To cut out carefully the motifs printed on fabrics and place them in a precise way results in an over-contrived design which owes its success or failure to the skill of the fabric designer. It has a parallel in the use of transfers for embroidery – a necessary aid in some cases but not fully creative. The arrangement of patches so that the pattern on one appears to continue on the next, serves to hide the method of construction, and this should not be attempted in any craft. Patchwork should have so much life and colour that it would be impossible to mistake it for a piece of printed fabric.

If we keep the direct approach of the early workers and use the best of our modern fabrics in the same unselfconscious way, some interesting work should result.

Equipment

Needles	These should be as fine as can be used successfully. The size should be related to the thickness of the thread.
Thread	Pure silk for silk fabrics. Nylon thread for fabrics from man-made fibres. Cotton for other fabrics, no. 40 to 100 according to the skill and eyesight of the worker. Black should be used for sewing dark patches together and white for light ones. When sewing light patches to dark ones, black cotton seems to show least. Tacking cotton (basting thread).
Scissors	Sharp pair for fabrics. Old pair for paper.
Paper	Strong paper such as that used for large heavy envelopes is good for beginners. Skilled workers find fairly thin notepaper of good quality most suitable. Thin white cardboard is only used for projects such as mobiles when it must be left in.
Vilene, or Pellon	This is good for bags and boxes instead of paper patterns as it can be left in as part of the padding.
Pins	Fine steel or brass.
Thimble	This is necessary for speedy and rhythmic work.
Templates	See pages 10 to 12.

Opposite
Big Flower
A simple wall-hanging using patches of slightly varying lengths and widths, cut from a wedge-shaped template. A single turning was made on one long side of each patch and this edge was placed so as to cover the raw edge of the next one. The patches were sewn down by machine. Thin sheet copper with beads and sequins wired to it were used for the centre. The top and bottom of the panel were finished with strips of brass about 1 cm wide and 2 mm thick. This is sold in some chain stores for the tops of pelmets.

After holes have been drilled in it at intervals, it should be polished and covered with clear varnish. It can be attached to the panel by means of stitches through the holes.

Materials

Most fabrics can be used for patchwork provided that they do not stretch or fray easily.

The larger the collection of both plain and patterned fabrics, the richer in colour and texture the results will be. The following materials are suitable:

Cotton: smooth or textured, dull or shiny, e.g. piqué, twill, sateen, strawcloth, cotton velvet, towelling, fabrics with slub weaves

Linen may be combined with cotton of similar weight

Silk and velvet may be used together

Fabrics containing lurex

Felt

Wool and wool and cotton mixtures

Fabrics from man-made fibres. Transparent ones will need a backing of similar fabric.

Rayons which stretch and fray easily should be avoided.

Note

The different fabrics used in one piece of work should be of similar weight. All creases should be pressed out before the patches are cut.

It is advisable to wash small cuttings if there is any doubt about the fastness of the dyes.

Pieces of old garments may be used if not weakened by wear or many washings.

Fabrics with naturalistic floral patterns and those with geometrical ones do not combine well.

Templates

Templates must obviously be completely accurate. They can be bought from the firms listed on page 96, but they can also be made as shown in the diagrams on pages 11 and 12.

Metal, perspex (plexiglas) or cardboard may be used. The latter is not suitable for large projects as the edges tend to wear away with the action of the scissors when the paper patterns are cut.

Metals can be cut with special shears, and cardboard with a sharp handicraft knife. A metal ruler, protractor, compasses and a set square are necessary.

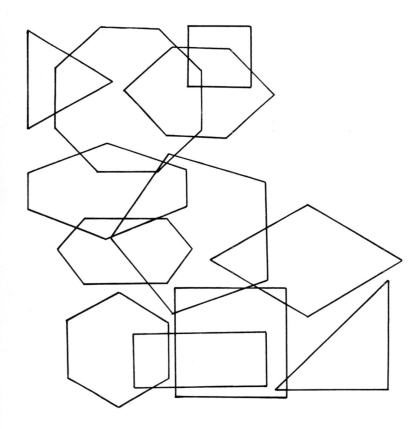

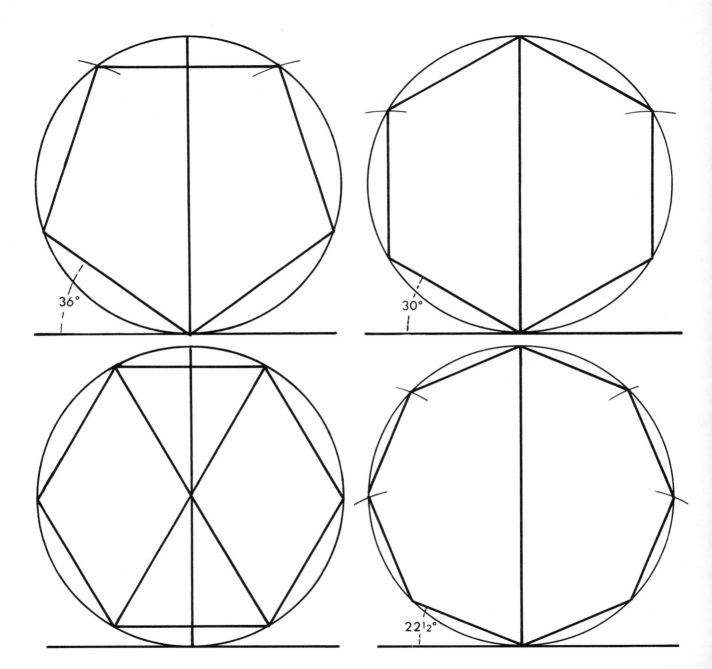

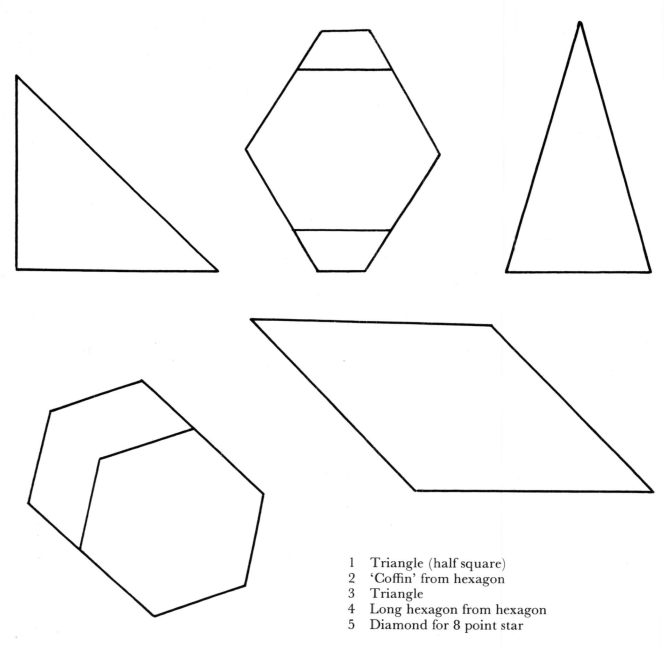

1   Triangle (half square)
2   'Coffin' from hexagon
3   Triangle
4   Long hexagon from hexagon
5   Diamond for 8 point star

Paper patterns

These are cut with the templates held firmly on the paper and with the scissor blades touching the edge of the template as they cut around it. They must be accurate.

It is good practice to cut paper patterns from the coloured and black and white pages of old magazines. These can be used to make decorative paper patchwork panels using the designs on pages 20 to 36 (see page 69 and example below). These panels make colourful classroom decorations.

Paper patterns, if taken out carefully, may be used several times.

Fabric patches

Pin a paper pattern to the wrong side of the fabric and cut a patch $\frac{3}{8}$ in. larger all round for seam allowance. If possible, place one side along the grain of the fabric.

Tacking or basting

Fold the seam allowance exactly over the edge of the paper and tack (baste) as in diagram. Leave the ends loose for speedy removal later.

Sometimes turnings must be tacked (basted) so that the stitches do not show on the right side. This is the case when fabrics show needle marks or when the patterns are to be left in. The seam allowances may then be cross-tacked (cross-basted) as in diagram 2, or corner tacked (basted) as in diagram 3, through the folds of the fabric only. In some cases, see pages 42, 43, 50 and 52, the turnings may be glued down with a latex adhesive.

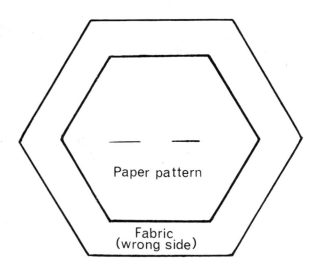

Paper pattern

Fabric
(wrong side)

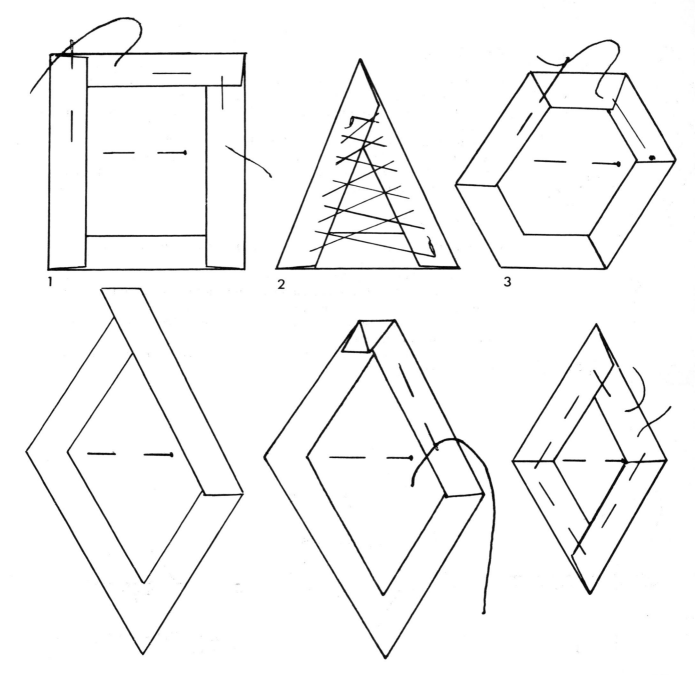

1

2

3

15

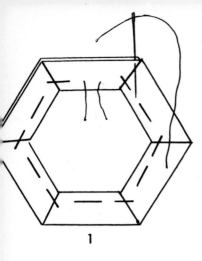

Seaming

Place two patches with right sides together. Take the first stitch through the front patch only, as near to the corner as possible (diagram 1).

Lay the end of the cotton along the top of the patches and seam over it from right to left (diagram 2).

To fasten off, work backwards for 4 stitches (diagram 3).

Sometimes several patches can be joined without fastening off.

When making a diamond star, seam from A to B and fasten off each time. This eases the fabric to the centre and helps to prevent a hole being left there.

Finishing off

When all the patches are sewn together, press on the wrong side. This helps to hold the turnings in place.

Take out tackings (bastings) and papers.

Press on the right side under a slightly damp cloth, stretching the patchwork gently at the same time. It is then ready for making up.

If the patchwork is pressed in this way there should be no ironing difficulties in subsequent launderings.

Patchwork should, even if soiled, never be washed before making up, as it might lose its shape.

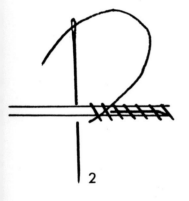

1

2

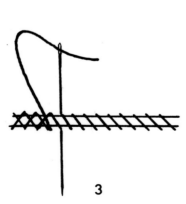

3

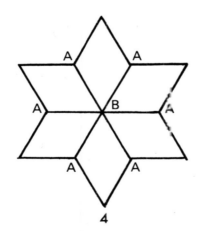

4

Ladder stitch— the edges are pulled together

Colour

The colour in patchwork depends on the fabrics which are available, but as these are plentiful today it is often possible to choose colours which fit in with a particular scheme and with individual preferences.

The following are ways of using colour in patchwork:

1 It may be necessary to use every scrap of fabric irrespective of colour. In this case the design must depend on tone relationships, though some attempt must be made to distribute the colour in an organised way (see colour plate facing page 72).

The tone of a colour is its lightness or darkness. For example, pale green or pale blue are lighter in tone than dark green or dark blue. In addition to this, some colours in their pure form are lighter than others; yellow is lighter than red or green, both of which are lighter than purple. Black and white may be regarded as the darkest and lightest tones respectively.

It is of the greatest importance in all patchwork design to consider tone relationships. If there is any doubt as to whether one piece of fabric is lighter or darker than another, they should be viewed in a half-light; the hues will then disappear and the difference or similarity of the tones will be seen.

2 A piece of printed fabric may have particular appeal and be the starting point for another type of design (see page 64). Here some fabric with a pattern in pink, red, blue, green and white on a yellow background was chosen first. Three more patterned fabrics of a less definite design were added, with four different plain yellow fabrics.

3 Restrained use of colour with fabrics of very different textures and of several shades of one colour can be most effective.

Opposite
'Many Doors' panel
This panel 4½ ft × 2 ft, is made of six large rectangular patches of furnishing fabrics in blues and greens on a background of dark blues. On each patch are smaller 'door' patches of various colours. All edges are left without turnings and secured by several rows of machine stitching, allowing the frayed edges to add to the texture and in some cases to the colour. There is some hand embroidery in silks, cotton and gold thread

Equal proportions of two or more hues or tones may be difficult to arrange so as to make a successful design. Experiments should be tried using varying amounts of each. The use of a small amount of vibrant colour will often have a dramatic effect. It is interesting to find out what happens when this colour is moved into a different context. Experiments of this type will teach something about the behaviour of colour.

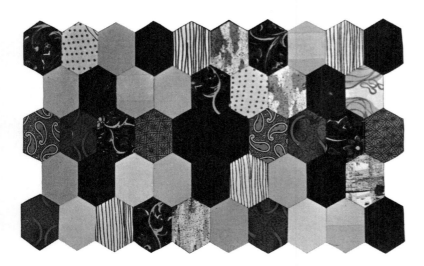

A subtle variety in colour is one of the characteristics of good patchwork. Much of the colour interest will be lost if all the same browns, or reds, or greens, are used in one piece of work. A good look at colour in nature will show that there are many different hues and tones in a hedge, or a ploughed field, or a flower, or even a single leaf. Patchwork is a good way of expressing awareness of this. If a large amount of one colour is needed, (for a background, perhaps) a number of different fabrics can be dyed together, and the slight resulting variations of colour will add a great deal of interest.

Much can be learned about colour and design from studying the works of great painters, and it is worthwhile to note the way in which colour is used in the stained glass windows in churches and cathedrals.

Pattern design

Many different stripes and motifs can be made by changing the positions of the dark and light patches. Ideas for patterns are shown in the following pages but these are by no means the only possible ones. When a number of dark, medium and light toned patches have been prepared they should be moved around on a sheet of brown paper or a cork mat until a pattern made by the different tones and colours has emerged.

They should then be pinned down, and can later be removed one at a time and sewn together in the right order. This will prevent the wrong placing of a patch which would confuse the design.

Motifs are sometimes placed at regular intervals in a design and so need other patches in between. These should be of a contrasting tone so that the motifs will stand out. 'Flowers' made from seven hexagons (pages 68 to 69) or long hexagons or 'coffins', and crosses made from five squares (page 59) can be joined directly to each other, but in this case, each motif should be of a different tone from the ones surrounding it.

Some designs, however, are not made from motifs, but are free arrangements of patches of different colour and tone (see pages 73 and 74 and colour plate facing page 24).

Stripes

Stripes can be wide or narrow, horizontal or vertical, diagonal or broken. They can be narrowly or widely spaced, and may have motifs at intervals between them.

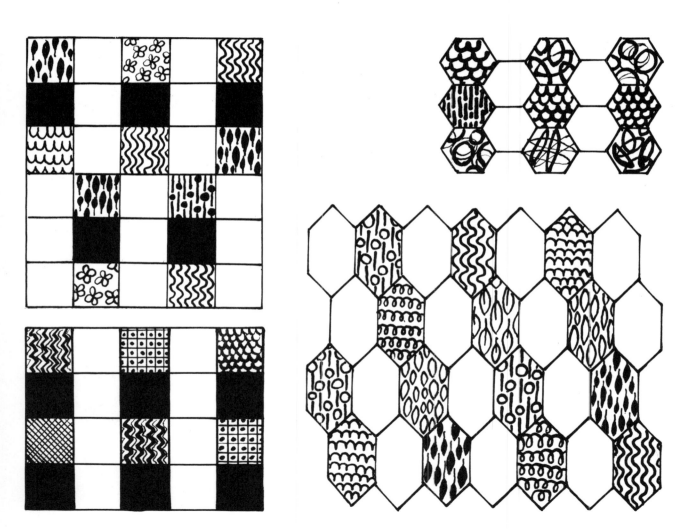

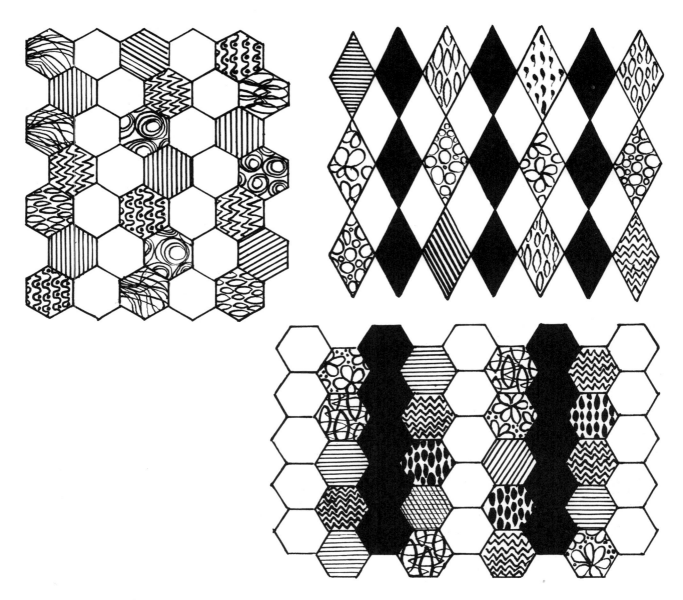

Hexagons

One hexagon surrounded by six others makes a 'flower'. A flower with twelve hexagons sewn round it is a 'double flower', while eighteen hexagons placed round a double flower makes a 'triple flower'. These diagrams show how different placings of the light, medium and dark patches can change the pattern.

Motifs can also be made with four hexagons.

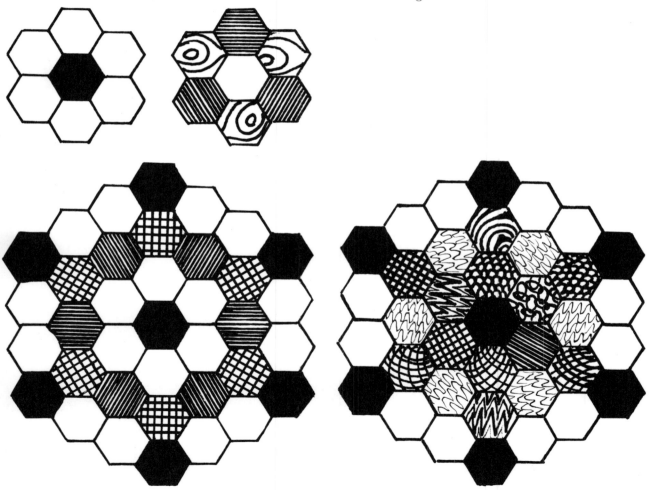

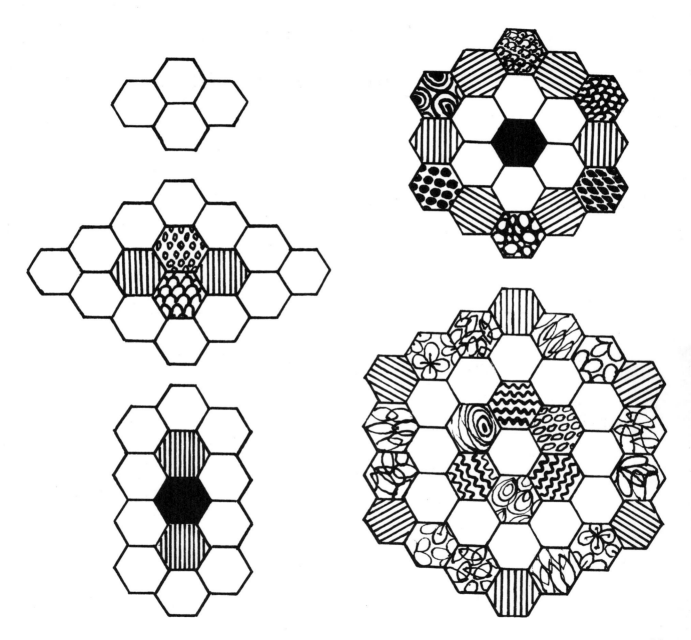

Squares and rectangles

Opposite
'Summer Time'

Abstract design in squares. The paler patches are in yellows, orange, pinks, light greens and browns, and the dark patches in dark blues and greens. It has a light navy blue background.

When using squares, it is a waste of time to sew together two or more exactly similar patches. It is more practical to use one large patch or strip in their place.

Triangles

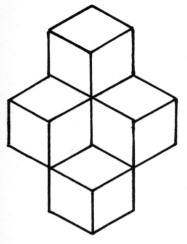

Diamonds

Diamond shapes can of course be varied in length and width. The one used in these patterns is one-third of a hexagon (page 11).

There are four ways in which they can be fitted together; box, trellis, zigzag and star. All the motifs on this page are made from the 'box' arrangement. Some appear to be three-dimensional, which tends to look disturbing on a flat surface.

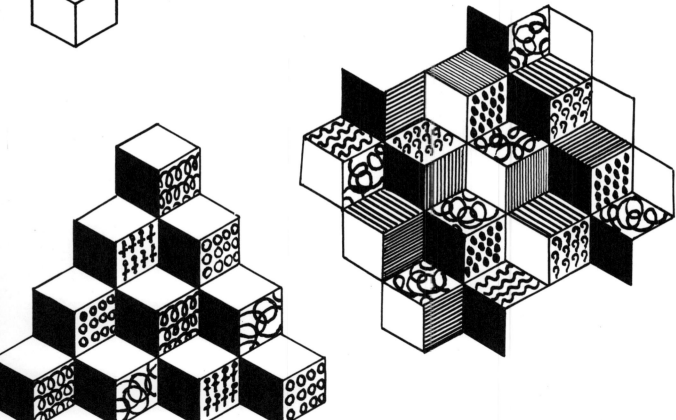

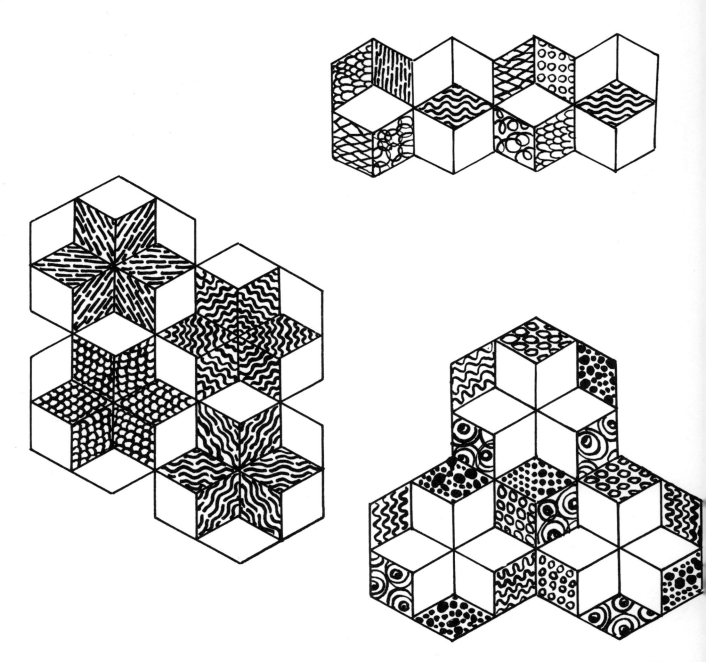

27

Stars

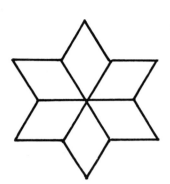

There are two star patterns which are usually made; the six-point and the eight-point star. The six-point is made from the hexagon diamond (page 11) while the eight-point uses the diamond shape on page 12 (diagram 5). The trellis and zigzag arrangements are also shown.

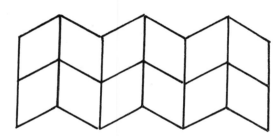

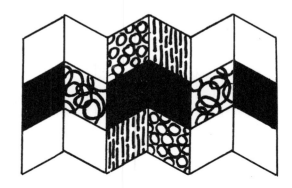

Hexagons and diamonds

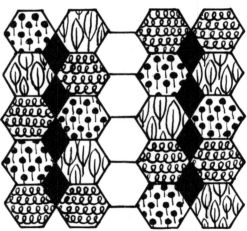

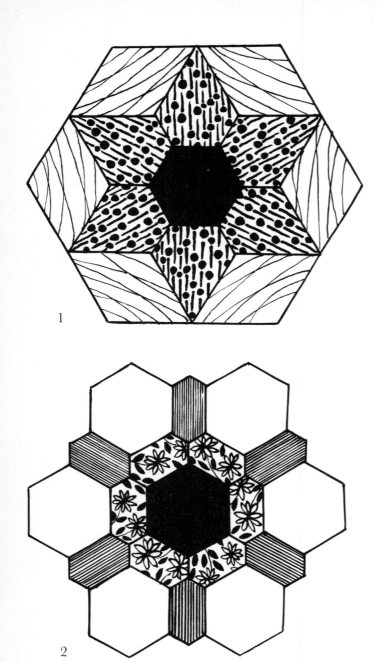

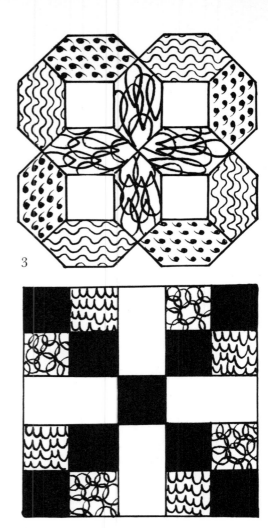

1 Pentagons, hexagons and diamonds
2 Long hexagons and hexagons
3 Long hexagons and squares
4 Squares and rectangles

32

5 & 6 Squares and octagons
7 Long hexagons and diamonds

Opposite
Hexagon flower pincushions
Make two hexagon 'flowers' with light centres and dark petals or dark centres and light petals or one of each. Place them together (right sides inside) and seam together leaving two sides open. Finish as shown on page 38.

The smallest pincushion illustrated ($\frac{1}{2}$ in. hexagon) is made into a wrist pincushion by sewing on an elastic band.

33

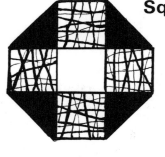

Squares and triangles

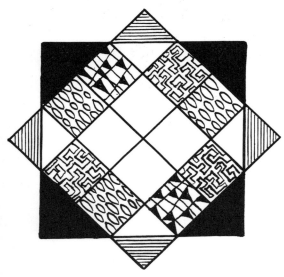

34

Sampler in cotton fabrics in purples, reds and pinks with touches of yellow and green

Hexagon surrounded by pentagons and diamonds

An arrangement of squares and triangles

Diamond star with hexagons

Border pattern in triangles

Pincushion or doll's cushion

Template 2 in. hexagon.

Prepare two patches (diagram 1), place the right sides together and seam together round five sides.

Take out tackings (bastings) and papers without disturbing the turnings. Tack (baste) round both edges of the open sides, (diagram 2). This is very important as failure to do so will make finishing difficult.

Turn right side out and stuff firmly with sheepswool, lambswool or unravelled wool. For a pincushion, sawdust or washed and dried tea leaves may be used if packed into a bag of the same size and shape. Tack the open sides together and close with ladder stitch or seaming. See page 16.

Prepare two 2 in. side hexagon patches (diagram 1) and six 2 in.× 1 in. oblong ones (diagram 3). Seam a long side of each oblong to an edge of one of the hexagon patches. Seam the short ends of the oblong patches together and finally sew on the second hexagon, leaving one side open. Finish as before.

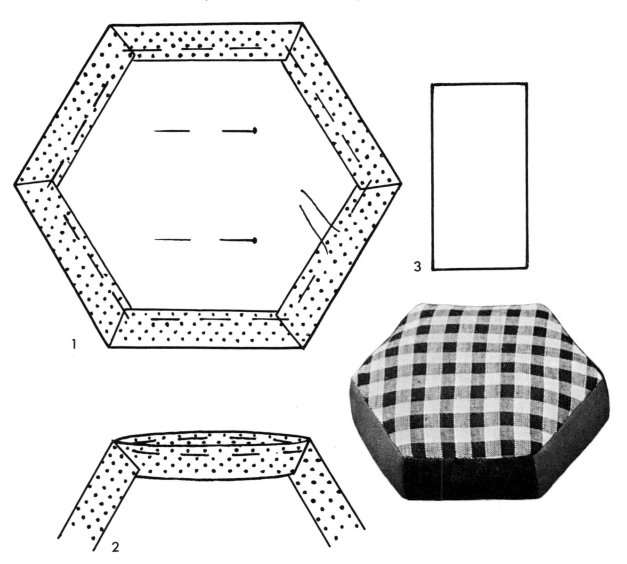

Cube pincushion

The square template can be of any size.

Cover six paper patterns, two dark ones for the top and bottom and four lighter ones for the sides. This can be varied.

Seam into a cube on the wrong side, leaving one side open, and finish as before.

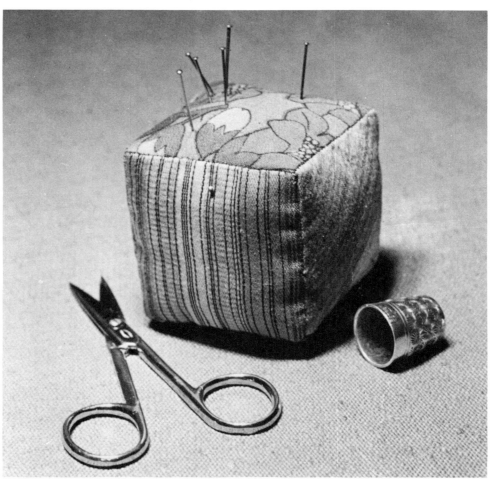

Bird

The body is made from two triangles and the legs and beak each from two smaller ones.

The pairs are sewn together, stuffed (with old nylon stockings) and finished as for pincushions. The legs and beak are seamed or ladder stitched in place and felt eyes are added.

Black Sambo

Each side is made separately of three black patches (head and legs) two white ones (collar), two gingham ones (sleeves) and 1 red (body).

The hair is made from rug wool sewn down in loops, and eyes and mouth are of felt.

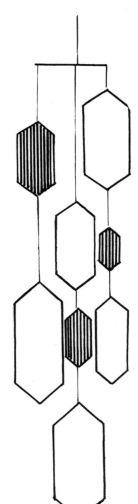

Mobiles

The units in these mobiles are each made of two patches or in the case of the diamond stars, two groups of patches sewn or glued together. The sizes of the units vary, so several templates will be needed.

Thin white cardboard is used instead of paper for patterns, and this is left in.

The finished units are suspended from a rod or lampshade ring with nylon thread, making sure that the balance is correct.

Mobiles from lurex fabric make attractive Christmas decorations.

43

Mobiles can also be made with three-dimensional units and many variations are possible.

Single units, suitably decorated, make interesting Christmas tree ornaments.

Mobile in lurex fabrics. Co-operative work of students at the Training Centre, Kirkham

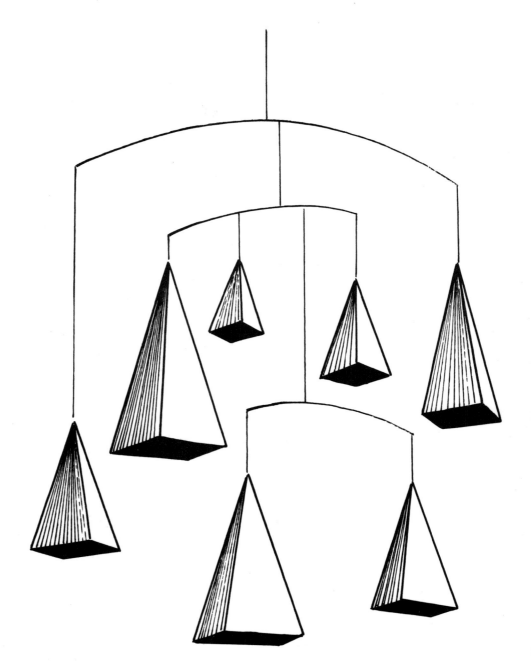

Balls

Prepare eight patches (four light, four dark) from template. Seam together, making sure that the points meet, leaving a gap of about 2 in. in the middle of one seam. Remove papers. Turn right side out and finish as pincushions.

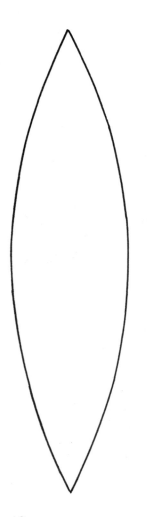

Prepare twelve pentagon patches. Seam five patches round one and join these to make half a ball. Repeat this with the remaining six patches, fit the two halves together and seam up, leaving two sides open. Finish as pincushions.

If felt is used no turnings are necessary.

See colour plate opposite page 81.

Place mats

One is all-over patchwork in hexagons and diamonds, and the second is a strip of five 2 in. squares seamed to the top of a square of plain fabric.
 Both mats are lined with a cotton fabric.

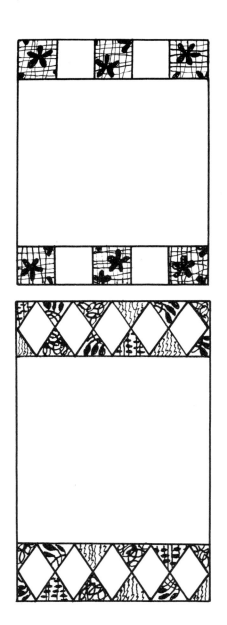

Boxes

Jewel box in lurex fabrics and satin.

    Make the lid first, as it will affect the size and shape of the box.

    Vilene (Pellon) can be used instead of paper for patterns.

    The base should be $\frac{1}{4}$ in. smaller in length and width than the top, and the sides will fit round this.

    The top should be padded and each section of the lining cut in Vilene (Pellon) covered with fabric, and glued or sewn in place.

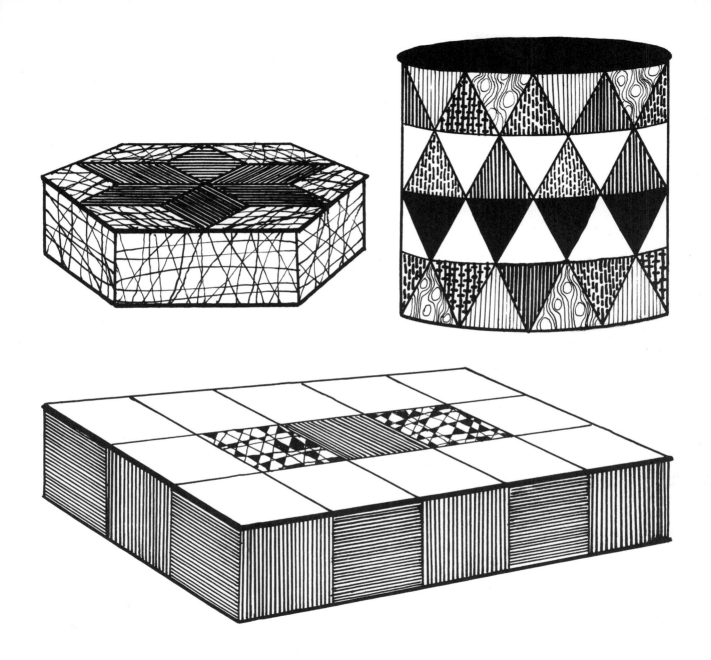

Bags

Bag made from lurex fabrics in dark colours, from twenty 3 in. × 1 in. patches and five smaller ones× 2½ in. × 1 in. The patterns are made from Vilene (Pellon) instead of paper, and are not taken out. The turnings are cross-tacked (diagram 3 page 15) or glued down with latex adhesive. When the patches have been seamed together, sew in a silk lining.

Fold as diagram and ladder stitch the sides together. Sew on a button and loop, and a length of chain.

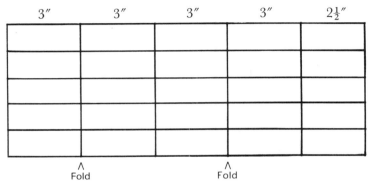

3″	3″	3″	3″	2½″

        ^ Fold   ^ Fold

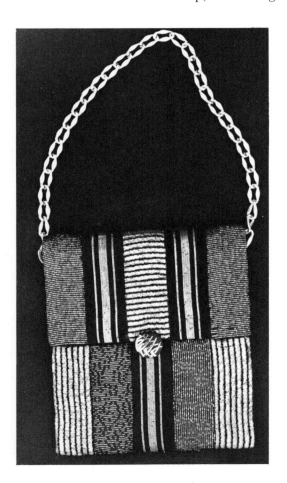

Knitting bag with lighter patches in greys and darker ones in many colours with reds predominating. The handles are attached as shown in the diagrams and the bottom is stiffened with a circle of cardboard.

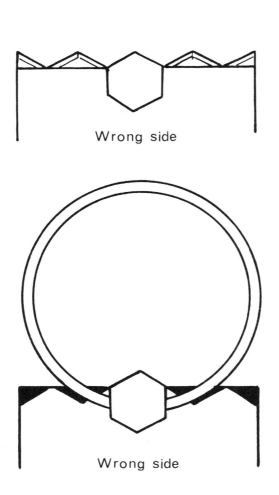

Wrong side

Wrong side

Cushions

Small cushion in 2½ in. squares made by Ita Caunce, age 9. The patterned patches are in reds, greens, yellows and orange, and the plain ones in browns and olive greens.

Five ways of making up

1 Seam the back and front together on the wrong side.
2 Open out turnings and backstitch the back and the front together on the wrong side.
3 Slipstitch a hand or machine-made cord round the seam.
4 Make back and front in continuous patchwork. Backstitch the two open ends together with a fringe between (page 55)
5 Make a piped join (page 60)

Bath cushion made from towelling in black and white, mustard yellow, orange and olive green.

The edge is finished with a twisted cord and rubber suction caps are attached to the tabs. As the cushion is filled with plastic foam chips, it can be washed and dried very easily.

Bath mats can also be made from scraps of towelling.

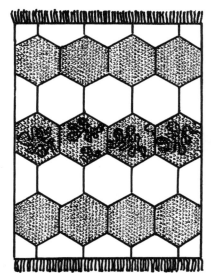

An idea for a beach cushion made in continuous patchwork. A cotton fringe makes a good finish for each end.

Opposite
A cushion based on a six point star made by Annie Barnes. Above is a design made with the same template but with the light and dark patches placed in different positions.

A flat cushion with 'coffin' shaped patches. The darker colours are royal blue, black, brown and purple, and the lighter ones tan and magenta with touches of purple, pink, blue and black. More plain than patterned fabric is used.

The pad is cut to shape from a sheet of plastic foam and covered with cotton. The back is made from two pieces of navy blue poplin over-lapping in the middle and the pad is slipped in under both pieces. The edge is piped in navy blue and is tied to the chair with tapes.

Cushion in hexagons and long hexagons. The light patches are in yellow and orange, and the centre one is in red striped with black. It is surrounded by light and dark olive greens and these colours are repeated near the edges, with some light red.

The striped fabric in browns, black, white and pale blue grey gives a frosted effect.

'Box' cushion in several shades of green with touches of blue and pink. The darkest cross is in reddish pink and pale browns.

The cover is easily removed for washing as it has a zip fastener sewn into one side.

The pad is foam plastic in a cotton covering.

Piping a cushion

Tack (baste) piping cord (pre-shrunk by washing) inside crossway strip $1\frac{1}{4}$ in. to $1\frac{1}{2}$ in. wide (diagram 1)

Starting in the middle of one side, place the raw edges of this piping along the raw edges of the cushion top, and pin. Leave about 3 in. free at the beginning and end for joining.

To join, cut the cord to the exact length needed and glue the ends together with a latex adhesive. Fold the ends of the bias strip so that the edges meet, pin press and sew together on the crease made (diagram 2).

Finish pinning in the piping, check to see that opposite sides are equal and tack all round. Snip the raw edges of the piping at each corner close to the stitches.

Tack on the piece for the back of the cushion (diagram 3 shows section), and backstitch or machine close to cord. Leave an opening for inserting pad.

For a round cushion, the piping must be snipped all the way round.

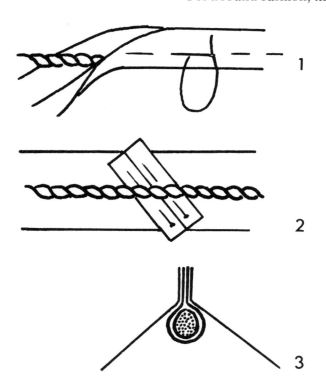

1

2

3

Permanent opening for cushion

Cut a straight strip of fabric about 2 in. wide and twice the length of the opening, plus $\frac{3}{4}$ in.

Pin this along both sides of the opening with the right sides together (diagram 1). Join the ends of the strip, and sew it to the opening $\frac{3}{8}$ in. from the edge.

Turn over the strip to the wrong side, make a single turning, and hem down (diagram 2). No stitches should show on the right side.

Fold the strip over to the inside. The dotted lines on diagram 3 show how it fits.

Sew on buttons and loops.

Square button $\frac{1}{2}$in.

Cut two pieces of heavy weight Vilene (Pellon) or other stiffening material $\frac{1}{4}$ in. square. Cover each with a piece of fabric 1 in. square (diagram 4).

Put the two together with turnings inside and ladder stitch or seam together. Sew on with shank (diagram 5).

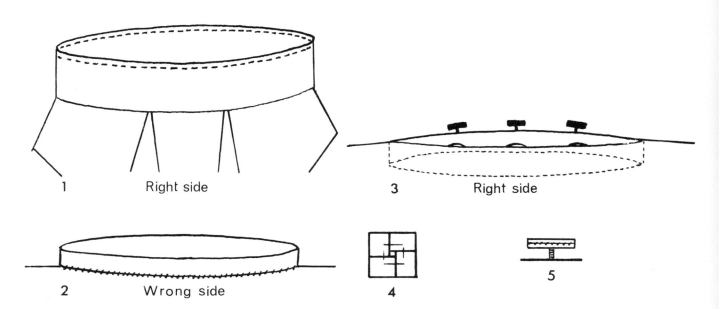

1   Right side

3   Right side

2   Wrong side

4

5

Two asymetrical designs with hexagons and diamonds which could be used for cushions or book covers. Designed and made by Jessie Doodson

Door sausage

This is made from woollen fabrics with alternate stripes of dark and lighter colours.

The patches are seamed together as shown in diagram. The end patches are joined so that the points meet and the sides are joined to make a tube leaving a 6 in. opening in the middle for stuffing.

This is made from pieces of old woollen garments made into a roll.

Tea cosy

Tea cosy in different yellows with touches of pink, reds and green. The squares are used diagonally and the pad is made from foam plastic.

Coffee cosy

Coffee cosy in white and pale greys with darker patches in tan, reds and green, purple, blue and olive green. More patterned than plain fabrics have been used.

Opposite
1 Rainbow colours in a rectangular cushion
2 A traditional double hexagon flower, fitting in with modern trends solely by its use of colour
3 One way of designing a cushion in squares

Doll's bed cover

Doll's bedcover made by Pauline Green, age 9.
A cotton lining $\frac{3}{8}$ in. wider all round than the top was cut, and a single turning $\frac{3}{8}$ in. wide was made on it. The wrong sides of top and lining were placed together, tacked, and joined with running stitch in embroidery cotton.

Motifs of similar size can be joined to make a repeating pattern, with the spaces between filled with patches of slightly varying tone and colour. Either lighter or darker patches than those used for the motifs will make the pattern stand out (diagram 1)

Motifs of varying sizes placed irregularly can also be joined in a similar way (diagram 2). Diagram 3 shows a detail of one such motif.

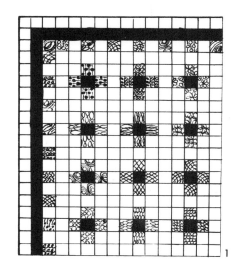

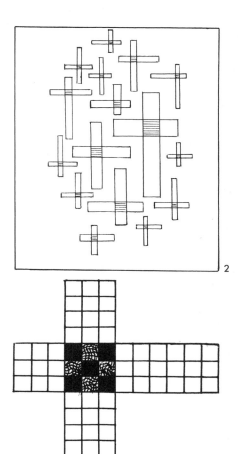

3

Bedcovers

Centre panel of a bedcover being made by Joan M. F. Louden. All patterned materials are being used.

Opposite
Paper patchwork design for a bedcover. The hexagon flowers fit together without intervening patches. Great care must be taken to vary the tones of the flowers.

Bedcover being made in a similar design by Annie Barnes.

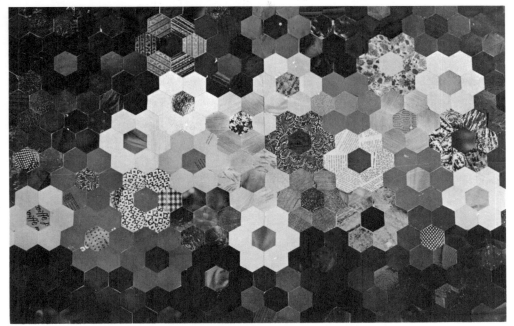

Finishing a bedcover

All bedcovers should be lined and the lining must be attached to the bedcover at intervals of about 6 in.

These are some ways of finishing the edges.

1 Bind with straight or crossway strip (straight seam binding or bias seam binding). The corners may be slightly rounded.
2 Pipe with cord covered with crossway strip (bias seam binding).
3 Join the top and lining with one or two rows of running stitch.
4 Cut the lining larger than the top and turn the surplus fabric over to the right side. Hem this down making sure that the border is the same width all round.

1 Bedhead panel in white and many colours by Jessie Doodson. The use of different tones in the triangular patches creates a lively pattern.

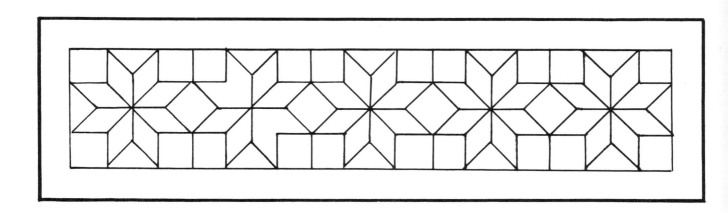

2 Any border design can be used to make a long narrow panel.

This bedcover is made up of triple flowers joined together with patches of light, dark and medium tones. Dozens of cotton scraps of all colours and a few bought remnants were collected. The way in which the colours and tone values have been treated should be studied. The lively sparkling effect is the result of using every available scrap whatever its colour, but arranging the colours and the tones in an organised way.

The cover is lined and the edges bound with a strip of navy blue fabric.

Opposite
Part of the bedcover shown on this page

Panels

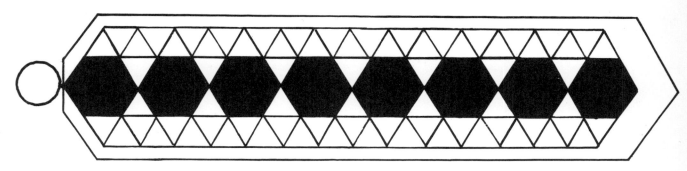

Another border pattern used in a panel.

Sunshine through Leaves
A small panel about 30 in. long, made of plain and patterned fabrics in greens, yellows, orange, browns and white.

'Across the Valley'
Panel in many colours in squares. Some of the squares are divided vertically or diagonally to suggest windows and gables. It is mounted on navy blue cotton and is $4\frac{1}{2}$ ft. long.

Creation
panel by Eirian Short
This depicts by means of symbols the creation of the world. The division vertically into light and dark tones denotes day and night; the circle is the world emerging from chaos. Simple symbols represent sea, growing things, Sun, Moon and Stars.

The panel is about $4\frac{1}{2}$ ft square.

74

'Sun, Moon and Stars'
panel by Eirian Short
This panel is almost 6 ft long and uses a mixture of fabrics, including some lurex. The centre of the sun and moon are slightly padded.

Patchwork appliqué

Single patches, or groups of patches can be sewn to a fabric background, and this may be a good way to make a beginning in patchwork.

The patches should be cut so that the grain of the fabric matches that of the background. Papers should be removed very carefully so as not to spoil the shape of the patches, which are then tacked in place and hemmed down as invisibly as possible.

Different sizes and shapes of patches may be needed in one piece of work, and the background chosen for them should be suitable in colour, tone and texture. Hand embroidery or machine stitching should only be added if it is necessary to link up different parts of the design or to achieve some desired effect.

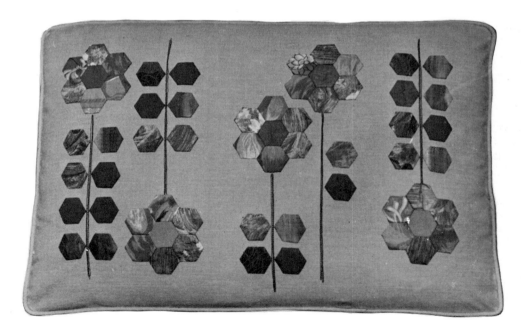

Panel with hexagon flowers in white, grey and black with touches of other colours. Each flower has its centre patch in a different red. The stems are tape of varying widths.

The background is grey, with shadowy stems and leaves in white machined lines.

Co-operative work of students at the Training Centre, Kirkham.

Hexagon flower in purple on a darker purple background made by Pauline Green, age 9. The flower is sewn on with running stitch.

Ideas for applied patches showing the use of striped and two tone backgrounds, decoration with stitchery and an arrangement of crosses made with squares of different sizes. The latter could be used in ecclesiastical work.

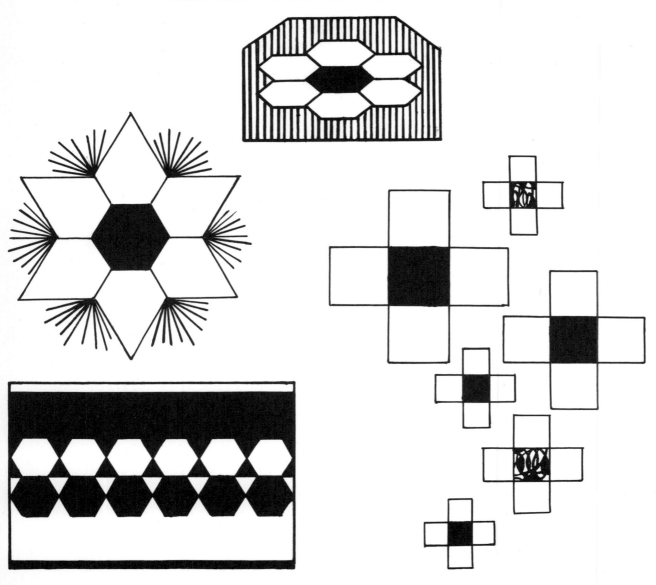

'*Projections*' by Eirian Short
An apparently three-dimensional panel approximately 36 in. square mounted·on hardboard. A mixture of fabrics in strong clear colours of green, pink, purple, yellow, orange and turquoise have been used. The way in which the dark and light tones have been placed has created the optical illusion

A patchwork design can be made by joining patches of many different shapes, but for this type a drawing must be made first. The designs on these pages may give ideas for this.

It should be remembered that straight sides are more easily sewn together than curved ones, and that there should be no angles which are difficult to manipulate when the fabric patches are tacked on to the papers.

When the drawing is completed, a tracing is made as a guide (page 83) and the original design is cut up and the pieces used as paper patterns. The patches are seamed together in the usual way. Tone values again are of great importance.

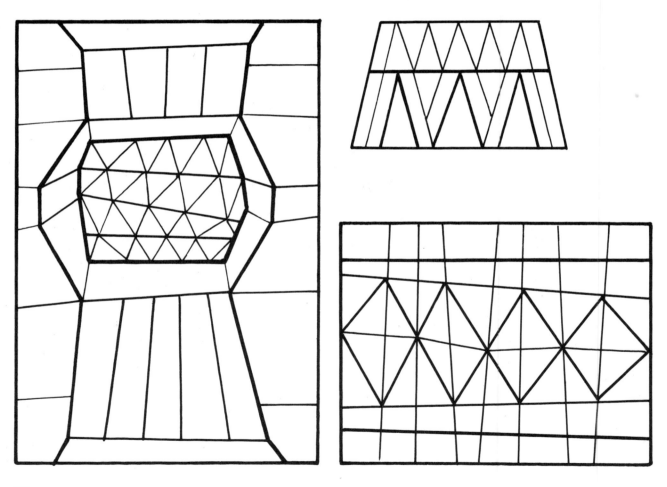

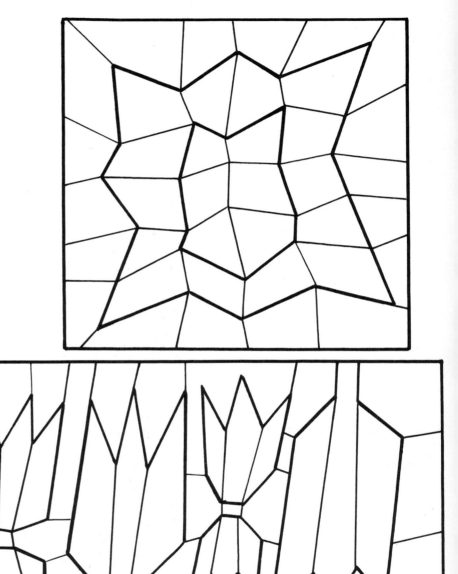

Large needle case with dark patches in navy blues and purples and the light patches in green, yellow green, and yellow. More plain than patterned fabric is used. The diagram gives another idea for a needlecase.

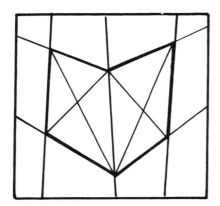

This shows the design for the needlecase on page 84 with arrows drawn in to show direction of thread.

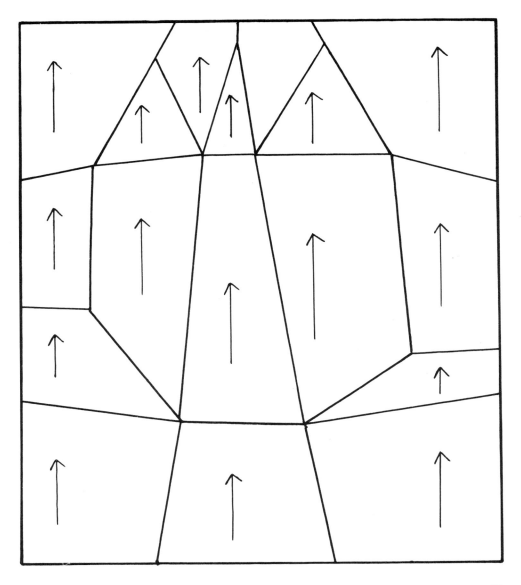

Tea cosy with triangles of graduated sizes in black and strong turquoise blue on a brown background. The edges are piped in black.

These are designs made with freely drawn patchwork shapes which can be applied to a background fabric. In this case there is no reason why the outer lines should not be curved, but it will be necessary to snip their turnings so as to make smooth edges.

Patchwork on the sewing machine

As it would be very difficult to machine patches together so as to make the corners meet precisely as in handsewn work, it is sensible to find a way of designing which is suited to the technique of machine sewing.

This cushion shows a simple way of machining together strips of fabric not all of the same width but of the same length, into panels (diagram 1). The seams are pressed open and the panels are machined together, again on the wrong side. When these seams are pressed open, the cushion top is complete.

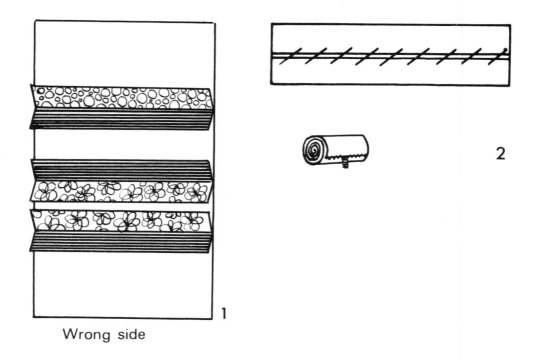

Wrong side

1

2

Cushion in plain and printed cotton in browns, yellows and orange with touches of many other colours in the patterned fabrics. It has a permanent opening with buttons and loops.

Button ($\frac{1}{2}$ in. long)

Cut a strip of fabric 1 in. wide and about 5 in. long. Turn the long sides over to the middle and catch together (diagram 2). Roll up very tightly from one end, make a single fold and hem this down. Sew on with a shank.

To make patchwork by machine in this way, first cut a paper pattern the size and shape of the finished article. Cut this into large sections (the square design on this page has five of these). Machine small strips together until pieces rather larger than each section are made. Press out the seams, and using the paper patterns, trim the pieces to the required size, allowing turnings. Machine these sections together.

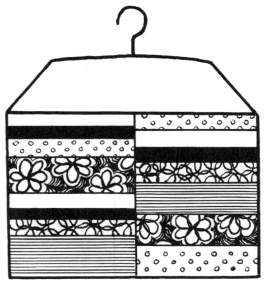

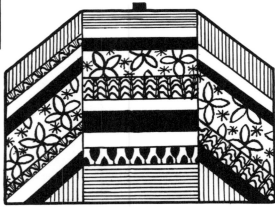

Circular box with machined patchwork side and plain brown top. The side is made of strips of brown, tan, royal blue, orange and burnt orange cotton.

This is a way of covering a ready made box of any shape. The lid should be detached.

First cover the lid with padding to fit and over it place a piece of fabric cut to size, leaving a seam allowance of $\frac{1}{2}$ in. Fold this over and glue it down.

For the sides, machine together enough strips (1 in. longer than the height of the side) to fit closely round. Turn over $\frac{1}{2}$ in. at the top and bottom and glue these turnings down. Snip them at the base so that they will lie flat. Glue a piece of felt over the base, and another one, $\frac{1}{4}$ in. smaller all round, on the underside of the lid. Cut pieces of felt to line the sides and base and glue them in place.

'*At the end of the road*' (left)
A mounted panel by Marjorie R. Timmins
Patches of very rich texture and colour were machined to a smooth background.
The effect of strong contrasts in tone should be noted.

'*Decorated Man*' (right)
Wall hanging with patches sewn by machine to a fabric with olive green warp
and blue-green weft. The frayed edges of this, against a background of black
velvet, give colour and texture interest. Some patches are of black velvet and
others of blue-black fabric which again is frayed to reveal a blue weft. The
surface is enriched with Victorian jet beads, braid, rug wool, and simple
stitchery in black Sylko 'Perle' or embroidery floss.

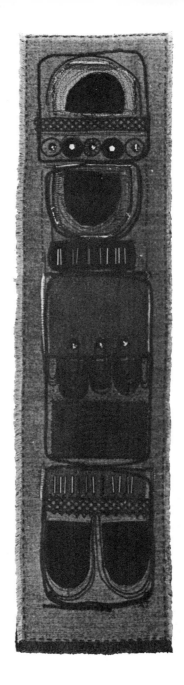

'*Quiet Village*' wall hanging. This has a background of patchwork in olive greens, browns and yellows. Rectangles of reds, dark blues and olive greens were machined to this to suggest doors, windows and chimneys, and details were added in straight and zig-zag machining.

Ideas for a panel of this type can be found in the walls of partly demolished houses, and in clusters of buildings.

Rectangular patches in browns, blues and blue greens were machined to a lighter brown background to make this panel. Much use was made of frayed edges. Embroidered bands raised above the background fabric may be used to emphasise movement or to add texture interest. Three examples are Portuguese border (2) raised stem band (3) and raised chain band (4). They are all worked on a firm foundation of stitches (1) which may be of any width and are generally, though not necessarily, covered completely with rows of stitches. These are worked on the foundation 'ladder' only and not through the fabric except when fastening on and off. The arrow in each diagram shows where the thread emerges for the first stitch.

For Portuguese border, the four stitches over the bottom two foundation stitches are worked first, followed by the left hand side. The work is reversed for the right hand side.

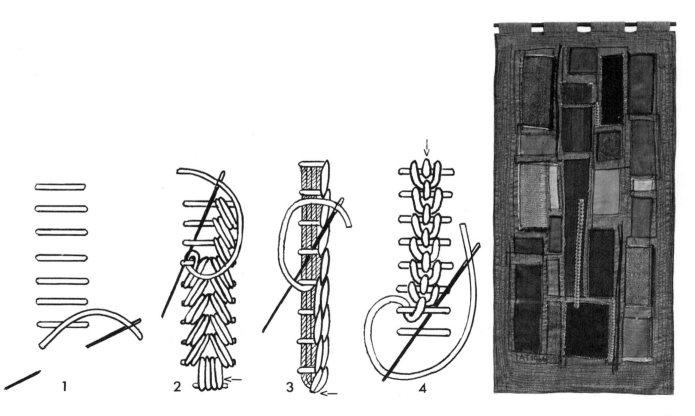

Suppliers

Templates

A. J. Scott Brook Street, Watlington, Oxon.
A. M. Row & Son Ltd 42 Market Place, Ripon, Yorkshire
The Needlewoman Shop 146-148 Regent Street, London W1

In the United States, templates (also called stencils) are widely available in art material supply stores.

Books

Patchwork Averil Colby, Batsford
Old Patchwork Quilts and the Woman Who Made Them Ruth E. Finley, Lippincot (USA)
American Quilts and Coverlets Florence Peto, Parrish
The Inward Vision Paul Klee, Thames & Hudson
Klee G. Di San Lazzaro, Thames & Hudson
Piet Mondrian M. Seuphor, Thames & Hudson
Stained Glass Windows V. Beyer, Oliver & Boyd
Stained Glass Robert Sowers, Zwemmer
Appliqué Stitchery Jean Ray Laury, Reinhold (USA)
Patchwork Quilts Averil Colby, Scribner (USA)
Patchwork Playthings M. Hutchings, Branford (USA)
One Hundred and One Patchwork Patterns Ruby S. McKim, Dover (USA)